D1315280

Found It!
Introducing Kids and
Families to Geocaching

Phyllis J. Perry

ISBN:1499691653

ISBN-13:9781499691658

TABLE OF CONTENTS

INTRODUCING GEOCACHING TO KIDS AND FAMILIES

A man, a woman, and a child stand by a bridge in a lightly wooded area near a meandering, shallow stream. But they don't cross it. The child looks among the rocks beneath the bridge at the edge of the water. The woman, slowly and methodically stares up at the underside of the bridge, now and then reaching up to feel along the top of the timbers with her gloved fingers. The man holds something in his hand. He goes forty feet away and slowly walks toward one side of the bridge, staring at the object in his hand as he moves closer and closer. He begins poking about in a bush.

The little girl finally leaves the rocks and moves to an old tree stump about ten yards away, not far from her father. She picks up a few loose pieces of wood shavings at the top and then suddenly squeals, "Found it!"

These three have succeeded at geocaching.

Introduction

This book is intended as a first introduction for kids and families interested in starting out to explore this new and exciting hobby called geocaching. Once you become an old pro at geocaching, you may want a lot more technical information and explanations. Then you'll need a far more scientific and detailed book than this one, and you can start your in-depth exploration with the bibliography of a few good references listed at the end of this book.

But as a non-expert myself, I offer to other beginners a fresh enthusiasm for this new sport and hope you'll find here simple and useful basic information as well as some tips that may be helpful to you in finding out more about geocaching. This introduction is guaranteed not to bog you down in complexity nor to discourage you from even getting started. While you won't have all the answers after reading this short book, your interest may be whetted and perhaps you'll end up with some exciting questions that you'll want to explore in greater detail.

What is Geocaching?

Have you seen the T-shirt that reads, "I Use Billion Dollar Satellites to Find Tupperware in the Woods. What's Your Hobby?"

Geocaching is a fairly new hobby that started in the year 2000. You might think of it as a combination of pirate treasure hunting, beach combing, and a little NCIS. You get to use maps, gadgets, and computers as well as your best detective and puzzle-solving skills. Adults and teens certainly geocache on their own, but it's also a fun activity that family members can enjoy together.

There are several variations on this theme, such as waymarking and terracaching but the term geocaching refers to the hobby or game as played by members of www.geocaching.com. This is the version to which this book refers.

Millions of people all over the world now take part in geocaching. Some recent statistics from the www.geocaching.com home page, which are always changing, show there are 384,280 active caches worldwide. In a typical recent week, 317,371 new logs were written by 44,751 account holders.

And it is a hobby that is growing very rapidly with dozens of new participants every day. Why? First of all, it's a lot of fun! Geocaching also has many side benefits. Solo, or as a family activity, it gets everyone outside moving about. Great exercise! Some of the areas where the searches take place are beautiful spots in parks or out in the woods where you can enjoy a hike, take some photos, observe birds, plants, and animals, and maybe even take along and enjoy a picnic lunch. Others are no farther away than your local shopping center and can add an extra dimension to an ordinary trip to the store.

Geocaching is also an educational activity. Everyone involved is going to learn something about maps, longitude, latitude, satellites, and computers. There'll be some math and some geography involved. The hiding spots for some caches may result in learning a little local history.

Some trips will encourage the use of a compass. Observational skills will be sharpened. Those seeking caches outdoors in wild areas will have the joy of getting up close to rock formations, interesting plants, and even animals. Suburban and urban caches may just take you to a lamppost in a shopping mall, but at its finest and most creative, caching will take you to interesting places you might never have known existed around the block or across town--or across the state/country--some on main drags, and some out-of-the-way, that you wouldn't have otherwise discovered.

And if you go geocaching as a family group, or with a few friends, there will be the added opportunity of learning to work together as a team. You'll also enjoy simple sociability as people with a shared interest spend time together.

Different Kinds of Caches and Many Choices

Geocaching is challenging and also offers a lot of choices. Each cache is rated on the Internet for the level of difficulty involved in finding it and also its difficulty level with respect to terrain. Some caches are located in remote areas that require a long hike. Others are close to spots that are only a short hike from where you can park a car. For "park and grab" caches, you barely leave your automobile or bike.

Caches may be in city parks or by a bridge over a freeway. They may be hung off trees or fences, and some cling by a magnet under a picnic table. The breadth of containers and types of hides is as wide as the creativity of the players. Every cache has the potential of being an old friend, or something quite new, challenging or simply laugh-out-loud clever.

If you have small children with you or if you are a young person or adult with limited strength or endurance, you might choose the easy or one-star difficulty terrains. (Note: one-star is often wheelchair accessible and 1.5 stars or even two stars are generally easy approaches.) Families of strong, active adults and teens may choose some caches that involve tough hikes and even rock climbs, if you wish. Don't be too

---

surprised though if on family outings, one of the little ones with sharp eyes turns out to be the one to first spot a hidden cache!

Caches abound for every type of cacher. Beginners probably want to limit themselves to a rating of no higher than two stars for terrain or difficulty until you get a feel for the game. But more on selecting caches in a moment.

Geocachers and "Muggles"

If this is your first introduction to geocaching, right now you are considered to be a muggle. (Many of you will recognize that name from the Harry Potter books and films.) Muggle is a name given by geocachers to refer to all those people who do not geocache. Geocachers tend to keep their treasure hunts secret from non-geocachers. If they are hunting a cache, and other people appear on the scene, the geocachers may simply wait until the muggles pass by.

You may already have been a muggle observing a geocacher without even knowing it. Perhaps you saw a person, holding something in his hand, walking toward a spot, and then stopping and examining a rock wall, tree, or boulder. As you passed close by, the person may have done nothing special or unusual and perhaps even sat down and looked as if he were just resting. But after you passed, when you glanced back, you saw him looking around again as if he were searching for something.

The only problem with muggles is that they know nothing about geocaching. If they accidentally come upon a plastic container with interesting items in it, they may carry off the container without realizing they have disturbed a geocache. Every cache should contain a note for just such an occasion stating, "You've come upon a geocache. Please leave it alone." The official wording for such notes usually includes, "To learn more, go to www.geocaching.com." But this, sadly, sometimes isn't enough. When a cache goes missing, geocachers say, It's been muggled.

While you are out hunting a cache, if a muggle does stop to ask if you've lost something, you might give a quick explanation of geocaching. Often the muggle is intrigued and offers to help hunt. Many, when they see that the treasure involved is nothing more than a plastic tub or a 35 mm film canister with a rolled-up piece of paper and a few trinkets inside, just shake their heads and move on. Others are interested. Most geocachers love introducing the sport to new people.

How to Geocache

Geocaching works like this. One person hides the cache, typically a small weatherproof metal or plastic container. Within this container you'll find a logbook and a pen, and perhaps some small, inexpensive trade items, little treasures, which are officially known as Swag. The person hides the container in a public-accessible place. Perhaps she will put it in the crotch of a tree or under some rocks, or magnetically affix it to the back of a sign. Perhaps she will hang it from the limb of a thick pine tree using a twist tie, or perhaps she'll push it out of sight into the crevice of a rock wall.

Using a global positioning system, the hider determines the location (called the waypoint) as close as possible in terms of its longitude and latitude. When she gets home and has access to a computer and the Internet, the cache hider enters that information about this newly hidden cache onto www.geocaching.com.

After she enters these waypoint numbers, and any

other information about the cache that she wishes to share, this cache is submitted for review. Someone from geocaching.com will review the listing for accuracy, for adherence to the site rules, for proximity to other caches, etc. Once approved, the new cache is published on geocaching.com (usually within a day or two), and it becomes accessible to other members of geocaching.com for finding.

Once it is posted, others looking on the Internet for caches to seek in their area can read about this new cache. These seekers, e.g., geocachers-- enter the waypoint into a GPS receiver. Using this directional information, the seeker goes out to try to locate the hidden cache. It may be the same day that the cache is posted, or it may be days, weeks, or months later. Cache listings remain active as long as the cache is maintained. Some are several years old. Others get retired or archived after only a few months.

When a cache is found, the finder first logs his/her visit by writing his geocaching nickname and the date of the find into the log book. Then he may choose to swap trade items. The finder takes out one of the little treasures or pieces of Swag and replaces it with another small trinket that he has brought along for just this purpose. At home, the finder uses his computer to call up that cache which has a name and number assigned to it on the geocaching website, accesses the cache page, and logs the find there by entering the information to show that he has found it..

Recording such a find is easy. Geocaching.com uses a simple online form with several options for logging a cache: Found it, Didn't find it, Write note, Needs Archiving, or Needs Maintenance. Most entries are a simple Found it. The cacher submits his log which becomes part of the cache page for future seekers and other visitors to read. It is emailed directly to the cache hider, and the find is noted on the cacher's account as a "smiley" or found cache.

—

Sounds easy enough, doesn't it? And it is. But by now, you probably already have a few questions. What is this GPS receiver, how does it work, how do you enter a waypoint into it, and how do you use this geocaching Internet site?

What Is the GPS and How Does a GPS Receiver work?

Satellites fly hundreds or even thousands of miles above the earth. High satellites travel about 7,000 miles an hour and the lower ones travel at more than 17,000 miles an hour.

Satellites need power, and most get this power from the sun. They have solar panels attached to them, much like the solar panels you may have seen on top of some houses and other buildings in your community. These solar panels gather energy from the sun, and they change it into electricity. The satellites carry with them instruments powered by this electricity,that can do different things. Communication between these satellites and earth takes place by the use of radio waves.

Almost two dozen countries in the world have sent up satellites to orbit our planet. The first was a satellite called Sputnik I which Russia sent into space in 1957. It was about the size of a basketball and weighed less than 200 pounds. The very next year, the United States sent up a satellite called Explorer I.

Over time, larger satellites have been shot up and are now used for many purposes. The navigational information from satellites is used by the Army and Navy. Some satellites provide information to help keep track of weather. Others transmit phone, radio, and television signals.

One group of satellites, called the Global Positioning System (GPS),was developed by the U.S. Department of Defense. Called NAVSTAR, the U.S. government's global positioning system was first used by the US Navy in 1978. The twenty-four satellites (plus spares) in this system each weigh about 2,000 pounds and reach about seventeen feet across. They move at over 8,000 miles an hour, travel about 12,000 miles above ground, and last about ten years. Each satellite orbits the earth once every twelve hours and follows one of six orbital paths. This system allows us to locate people and things all around the world.

At one time the information from the Global Positioning System was only used by the military and by other people with security clearances. Finally a civilian version became available but it had slight inaccuracies. This slightly watered down version was called selective availability (SA). It was accurate only to about 300 feet. In May 2000, President Bill Clinton passed an executive order telling the military to remove the SA feature, thus making it accurate to around thirty feet. From that time on, anyone with a GPS receiver could use the information from these orbiting satellites to locate a point on Earth with great accuracy.

Three Parts to a Global Positioning System

A GPS has three parts. The space segment refers to the actual satellites orbiting Earth. The control segment includes the people and equipment that launch and man the ground stations that control these satellites. Crucial information, including its position in space, is uploaded to each satellite from the ground. Finally, there is the user segment. This refers to those who are using GPS receivers. One of these receivers which is about the size of a cell phone, can be held easily in a person's hand. It's really a special kind of radio-receiver and computer designed to give people information about their precise location on Earth.

Each GPS satellite carries four atomic clocks so that all the GPS satellites operate with the same time reference. A satellite's message includes its identity, its location, and the time at which the signal is sent. This information is continuously sent by radio signals. A GPS receiver determines its distance from a satellite by measuring the time it takes these signals, moving at the speed of light, to travel from the satellite to the receiver. A GPS receiver will use signals from three or more of the closest satellites to figure its specific position based on its distance from these satellites.

Radio waves do not travel well through thick or metallic walls, and for this reason, you may not be able to use a GPS receiver inside your house. It can only be used properly outdoors, and even then, being in a deep canyon or beneath a canopy of thick trees can interfere with receiving the radio waves.

Different Kinds of GPS Receivers

To be a successful geocacher, your will need a GPS receiver. More than a hundred kinds are available, with lots of different features. Before buying one, you may want to consult with another geocacher and even try out a few to see what you'd like and what you can afford. Basic GPS receivers cost around one hundred dollars, but those with extra features may cost more than six hundred dollars. Some of these have special antennas that work better than most under dense tree cover and/or in narrow canyons. Marine versions are waterproof and float. (If you plan to cache and kayak, you might consider this.) Some have extensive mapping capabilities. Others are built to hold up better during rain and snow. Some have altimeters and digital compasses built into them.

Although this books talks about using a dedicated GPS receiver, some geocachers prefer to use their smart phones or other devices.

Wide Area Augmentation System

Many GPS receivers can read additional signals that are sent via the Wide Area Augmentation System (WAAS). This is a system of satellites and grid stations that provide GPS signal corrections to improve accuracy. At the present time the Federal Aviation Administration and the Department of Transportation are further developing the WAAS system to use it for flight approaches at airports. The WAAS system corrects for signal errors due to ionospheric disturbances, timing, and satellite orbiting errors.

The WAAS system includes 25 grid stations across the United States which monitor GPS data. Two stations on the coasts collect data and create a correction message which is then broadcast through one of two geostationary satellites with a fixed position over the equator.

When you're buying a GPS receiver, you might want to see if it is one that can read WAAS correction signals. Such signals are currently available only in North America, although other countries are developing similar systems. They work best in open areas and can improve the accuracy of your GPS in locating exact positions.

Things You Might Want With You GPS Receiver

Unlike cell phones, most GPS instruments used in geocaching do not transmit radio signals; they only receive them. For about one hundred dollars, you can buy a GPS receiver without extra bells and whistles that will work quite well for general geocaching purposes. Each receiver will come with a manual which you will want to study carefully.

You might also want to consider purchasing some GPS receiver accessories.

These are not essential to geocaching, but might be very helpful to you. You might, for example, want to use a computer connection cable to upload and download waypoints and routes between your GPS receiver and your computer rather than entering them all by hand. You might want a case for your GPS instead of simply tossing it loose into your backpack or your car's glove compartment. Screen projectors and mounts, or cradles are convenient for holding the GPS receiver while you're driving or kayaking or biking.

GPS Vocabulary

The GPS receiver has a vocabulary associated with it, and you will need to get familiar with some of these words. Five are particularly important. A pair of coordinates of longitude and latitude define your position on the earth. The coordinates displayed on your GPS receiver when it is tracking three or more orbiting satellites is called your position fix. When this position fix is given a number, name, or symbol, and is stored in the memory of your GPS receiver, it is called a waypoint. GPS receivers will let you store hundreds of waypoints or locations in them. Bearing describes the direction of one waypoint to another or the direction from your current position to the position of a waypoint. A heading describes the direction you are moving or facing. The GPS receiver also has a Go To function, which allows you to choose one of the several waypoints you have stored in your GPS receiver so that you can be directed to that particular location.

Once You Have Your GPS, How Do You Get Started?

Once you've picked out your new GPS receiver and studied its manual, you'll be eager to get started at finding a cache. What do you do first? Using a computer, the geocacher must go to a geocaching website on the Internet and choose one or more caches to seek.

The largest website is www.geocaching.com which is the one I'll be referring to throughout this book. Other major sites are Navicache.com, Brilling.com/geocaching, and TerraCaching.com. As you explore this new hobby, you may wish to visit a variety of web sites to see what they each have to offer. At www.geocaching.com, there is no cost for using the basic level of service. If you find you like this hobby, you may want to look into the Premium service, which is about the price of a yearly magazine subscription. It offers some useful tools for the frequent cachers.

When you click on the geocaching website, you'll find several options. You can click to read online to learn more about geocaching, highly suggested if you're a first-time user. You can scroll down to Create an Account where you will be given an opportunity to select a geocaching name for yourself. Some people use their initials, some use a nickname. This account will track all of your geocaching statistics: finds, cache hides, travel bugs, etc..

Choosing a First Cache

Armed now with a GPS receiver and your online geocaching account, you're ready to log on and select that first cache! The two most popular ways to seek a cache are to search by zip code or by home coordinates. Using your zip code, which is the commonest choice for beginners. Log in to geocaching.com. On the home page, look for the spot to fill in your zip code. Enter it. You will see a list of geocaches in that postal area.

You can also search by your home coordinates. When you set up your GPS receiver, take a waypoint of your own house. Follow the directions in your GPS receiver manual to do this. Once you get this accurate longitude and latitude, write down this information and save it. You will then have these home coordinates handy. When you are ready to seek a cache, log in to your account. The page that appears is called My Account Details. You'll also see a box called Search Options. Click on Update Home Coordinates. Enter your coordinates and click Mark as my home coordinates. Return to the My Account Details page. Under Search Option, click on Search for nearest cache from your home coordinates.

You'll get a list starting with the closest cache.

If you use the zip code method, the distance given for each hidden cache will be its distance from the local post office that serves that zip code. If you use the My Account home coordinates method, the distance shown will be from your house. The caches will have names and numbers, and they will be rated in terms of difficulty of the terrain and of finding the cache, with one star being easy, and five stars being hard.

Click on one of the nearby caches. Its cache page will appear on your computer screen. Read the description and decide if this is the cache for you. There may be a few sentences saying this cache is in a park area with picnic tables. Or it may say you would be wise to bring gloves to remove this cache from its hiding place. If you want to hunt this cache, print out this page with its information about the name of the cache, its number, waypoint, map, and any other information. Most new cachers should start with caches of one to two-star difficulty and terrain. Beginners should also start with Traditional Caches as opposed to Mystery or Puzzle Caches, Multi-Caches, or Virtual Caches, which will be discussed later in this book..

If your GPS receiver has the capability, and you have the skill, you can enter this cache page information from the computer directly into your GPS receiver. Or, you can print out the information on your computer printer and enter by hand the coordinates given for each waypoint into your GPS receiver The standard geocaching format for expressing longitude and latitude is in degrees and minutes with decimal fractions of minutes. This is probably the default format in your GPS receiver, but check your manual to be sure.

Geocaching web sites other than www.geocaching.com will have their own similar navigation menus for you to follow.

Hints for the Hunt

Now, with the cache waypoint in your GPS receiver, and having studied the cache page and downloaded a map and any hints you want to use, you are ready to go out and try your luck at finding a cache.

Step one is to decide what to bring. You'll certainly need your GPS receiver, a pen or pencil (sometimes the pen in the cache doesn't work), extra batteries, and Swag.

Do you need a bottle of water, compass, hat, jacket, lunch, etc?

Step two is to get close to the general area in which the cache is hidden. You may walk, bike, or travel by car. If you know, for example by having looked at the map on the cache page, that you are going to drive to a shopping center in the middle of town, you do not need to turn on your GPS receiver, and use up batteries, you can simply drive to the center and park and then turn on your GPS receiver.. If you're going to drive to a trailhead or visitors' center and then hike into the woods, or bike to a city park, you really don't need to turn on your GPS receiver until you reach that starting point for your search.

When you get as close as your knowledge or map allows, it's time to turn on your GPS receiver. You'll need to wait about one minute while your receiver connects with at least three orbiting satellites. Then activate the GoTo function for the chosen waypoint in the manner explained in your GPS receiver manual. If you're going by car, and you are close to the site, have your traveling companion place the GPS receiver on the dashboard facing up to the window as you approach your destination. If you're alone, pull off the road while you do this. Don't try to drive your car or pedal your bike and operate your GPS receiver at the same time. It is too distracting.

A screen (page) on your GPS receiver will indicate by an arrow the direction of the cache from your current position. It will give the distance, at first in miles, then in fractions of miles, and later in feet, as you get closer and closer. Remember that a GPS receiver will show you the shortest and most direct path to an object. Since you are on foot, bike, or car, you might need to go around a city block, follow a curve in the road, or walk around a cliff or pond. Your actual route to the cache will probably not be in a straight line.

Track a Route Back

If you are hiking to a cache, it's a good idea to take a moment before starting out to select the mark button on your GPS receiver to store your current position in it as a waypoint. You should always do this if you're going far enough to be out of sight of your car or bike. Why? After you have wandered about in your search, you may become confused as to where you are. Even city parks can be thick with trees and twisty little trails. This stored waypoint will guide you right back to your starting place. It doesn't take long to enter and can come in very handy if you go off a trail or get turned around.

Alternately, you can retrace your steps using a track log. Most GPS receivers have a track log feature that can be programmed to mark automatically your position at set intervals, such as every ten minutes. This creates a digital record of how you got where you currently are, and can be followed to take you back to your starting place. See your GPS receiver manual on how to save a track and do a track back or reverse route.

Closing in on the Cache

When your GPS receiver indicates that you are within 500 feet of the cache, you follow the arrows on your receiver and you walk toward the hidden cache. With three or more satellites functioning, the GPS receiver in your hand will guide you closer and closer to the cache. Try to walk at a regular pace, holding your GPS receiver in your hand facing up to the sky. You may be going to a park and grab cache very close to your parked car or bike. Or you may be in for a long hike. Most caches are hidden close to trails, so especially as a beginner, if you find yourself wandering far afield, carefully check your GPS readings again.

If you have chosen a traditional cache, you will be looking for a physical container. Traditional caches are classified as large, regular. (about 8 to 10 inches square), or small (soap holders or metal or plastic containers that are 3 to 6 inches.). A micro cache might be in a film canister or magnetic key holder, or something even smaller. A nanno cache is even smaller than a micro. Caches will be discussed in more detail in a later section.

Once you are within twenty feet of a cache, you need to rely on your detective skills. Look sharp! Use what you already know from reading the page at home about the cache. Size will make a difference as to where the cache may be hidden. Knowing the approximate size of the cache helps you carefully to check out your target area. Is there a hollow in a tree trunk? Is there a rock wall with niches in it? Is there a mound of loose rock on the ground, known to geocachers as a UPR (Unnatural Pile of Rocks)? Is there a nice thick bush right where your GPS arrow is pointing? Caches are not buried in the ground, but the cache is probably camouflaged or hidden. Does anything look out of place?

Remember, even when things like trees or buildings aren't in the way of your satellite reception, your GPS

---

receiver can take a moment to function well. Walk in a straight line at a steady pace near the spot where you know the cache is hidden. (If you walk slower than two miles per hour, you may get false directions.) As you walk, hold the GPS receiver in your hand with its screen facing up to the sky while you watch the arrow and the distance reading. In which direction should you be walking? Are you getting closer or moving farther away?

Often you will get changing and conflicting indications of the direction and distance to a cache. This is due to imperfect signal reception for various reasons, most of which are beyond your control. Get the clearest view of as much sky as possible and wait a while. Maybe the satellites will move into more favorable positions. Meanwhile walk back and forth a few times and also check out slightly different areas. Give each persistent indication on your GPS receiver serious attention.

Sometimes the coordinates are just off. People who hide caches aren't always perfect. They might have mis-entered the coordinates or taken a bad waypoint to begin with. So if you don't find the cache within ten feet of where you think it should be, spiral out from ground zero to twenty feet. Don't give up easily and stop searching. Remember that geocachers are clever, and they'll try to challenge you.

A Few Examples

Let me give you just a few examples that baffled me. The lid of a container of one cache that I found beneath a long log had been glued to another cut-off section of wood that was resting right under the log. Great disguise! From the top, it looked just like a piece of wood. One film canister cache that I found was attached by a plastic tie to the top of a clothes hanger that was hidden in a crevice in rock wall.

Thinking this was an odd place for a coat hanger, I pulled on it, and up came the film canister. One cache was hidden inside a metal box that was attached by a magnet to the foot of a light pole so that it looked like an integral part of the pole. As I felt beneath the box, it came off in my hands! Once my GPS receiver kept pointing to a sprinkler head in a park lawn. On closer examination, it turned out that a cylindrical cache had been glued right underneath the fake sprinkler head.

Coded Hints and Clues

If you can't find the cache, all may not be lost. There might be coded hints on the geocaching page you printed. Some people like to use these, and others don't. You can have the computer decipher a coded message for you before you leave home, by clicking on (Decrypt) which follows the heading Additional Hints. Or you can do the simple alphabetical letter substitution yourself. The key to reading the coded message is printed right on the page. The last thirteen letters of the alphabet are printed directly under the first thirteen letters of the alphabet. To read the coded message, you simply substitute the letter of the alphabet that is directly above or below the letter given.

For example: Use this code given below to decrypt this message.

Trbpnpuvat v f   s h a.

A B C D E F G H I J K L M

N O P Q R S T U V W X Y Z

If it's so simple, why even use a code? It prevents those

who don't want to use clues from accidentally reading them. And some of us just like to read and write coded messages! You'll learn more about Puzzle Caches later on.

Clues may be vague or specific. They might tell you that a magnet is involved or that you should look for a coat hanger hook in a rock wall. To help you find a canister hanging from the limb of a fir tree, the clue might say "think Christmas" which might cause you to think of ornaments hanging from tree limbs. Use these hints or not, as you wish. Some geocachers turn to these hints only when they have searched hard and failed. Some of us beginners like to start out with all the clues we can get! Remember too, that the title of the cache may provide a clue. Also, comments in the posted logs of previous finders may give you some helpful ideas. That's why, if you like to use clues and hints, it's important to read these at home before you start on your hunt. They may even have suggested a correction to the coordinates that were originally posted.

Suppose, in spite of your best efforts and using all available clues, you still can't find the cache. What then? Walk off a distance and approach again. Note where the arrow on your GPS receiver is pointing and identify in your mind a landmark in that direction. Walk off to the other direction and approach again. Watch that arrow and identify another landmark. The point where the paths of your two different approaches intersected is a good spot to examine very closely

What to Do Once You Find the Cache

Most of the time, with diligent search, you will locate a hidden cache. Hurrah! Success! Open the container, take out the notebook, and log in your geocaching nickname and the date of your find. Choose a piece of Swag to take and replace

—

with an appropriate trinket that you have brought along. (Because some caches are small, Swag must be small, too. In fact some micro and nanno caches are so small that only a tiny coil or paper is within, so you do not take away or leave Swag.) Now be sure to CAREFULLY put the cache back as you found it. Don't try to improve on it or move it. Be thoughtful of the next person.

Stop and revel for a moment in your success. Maybe even plan a delicious ice cream treat or some lemonade to enjoy on your way home. You deserve to celebrate great hunting.

But wait! You're not done yet. You need to go home and log your find on www.geocaching.com. Go into How to log a cache. Read what should be in your log, or check on what other geocachers have written in logs. You may choose to add a hint to help the next geocacher, but don't give too much away. Since the cache hider went to some trouble to put it out there for your enjoyment, it's nice to write a comment and give something back.

And what if you didn't succeed? When you simply can't find a cache, you record that fact, too. When you are back at your home computer, go to the geocaching website, call up that cache, go to log your visit and choose "Did Not Find." Maybe it simply wasn't your lucky day. Maybe the hider didn't do a good job of accurately recording the location. Perhaps a muggle found the cache and took it away. If you check that cache again on the web site after a few days or weeks, you'll be able to see if someone else found it and recorded the find. Or others may report that they can=t find it, either. My own first "Did Not Find" was not found by anyone else after the date when I failed to find it. Maybe it simply isn't there any more. Or maybe I'll find it if I get out that way and try again.

It's frustrating to be flummoxed. This is where knowing other geocachers is helpful. You can talk with other geocachers about your Did Not Find and maybe get some hints or clues. Sometimes the person who originally hid the find will send you an email when you report that you Did Not Find it. That person may give you a hint or report that the find has been muggled. Some areas have a volunteer who is the geocaching hot line. You may find this person by seeking out a local group or attending a special geocaching event and getting to know other geocachers.

Different Caches and What You Might Find or Buy

All caches are not the same. There are traditional caches, multi-caches, virtual caches, and puzzle caches.

Traditional Caches

As a beginner, you probably start by searching for a traditional cache. A traditional cache is an actual container of some kind that holds a small log book, a pen or pencil, and usually some Swag, small trading items. If you're adventurous, don't be put off by the word traditional. Each cache has its own surprises. It might contain a geocoin, a small disposable camera, information sheets about the historic importance of the site, a cache card with the name of the owner, a travel bug, etc. I've discovered all of these in traditional large or medium-sized caches.. Some of these container items will be discussed in more detail later.

One traditional cache I found contained some historical data. It held laminated sheets from a newspaper article detailing a plane crash that occurred at this spot when a slurry bomber was fighting a fire in this wooded area of Colorado. In such a cache, you sign the log, read the information, and replace the historical information safely back in the cache.

In addition to large and medium-sized traditional caches, there are some that are best described as small, micro, or even nanno A micro cache may be hidden in an empty 35 mm film canister, or in a metal or plastic pill holder. Nanno caches may be capsules small enough to be hidden inside a cigarette.

Geocachers can be very creative. Sometimes micros have magnets attached to them, so they can be attached to a guard rail, beneath a public telephone, or under a bench or picnic table. Some micro caches and nanno caches are so small that the page listing the cache may suggest that you bring along tweezers to remove the log sheet! You probably would not want to try seeking one of these for your very first geocaching trip.

Multi Caches

Multi caches require you to go to more than one spot. Using the original waypoint numbers that were given, you find a cache, and it contains a new set of numbers or provides a way for you to get another set of numbers. You enter these new numbers into your GPS receiver and go to that site. Here you may find yet another set of numbers, leading you on, leg by leg, to the final spot where you will find the hidden cache. The most famous multi, GCKGF2 9/8/2004 has over 100 legs! A multi-cache in Ketchikan, Alaska takes you to three totem poles.

One multi cache that I found had coordinates that led me to a statue. The cache page gave me a set of numbers that I had to combine with dates given on the statue, to get another set of coordinates. I followed these and walked a mile or so away to find the actual physical cache.

Mystery or Puzzle Caches

Sometimes the creator of a cache turns it into a Mystery or Puzzle Cache. You are given a waypoint to find a cache, and when you find it, there will be more directions helping you to solve a puzzle and find the next cache. Maybe you'll be told to look for a specific landmark such as a tree of a giant boulder. Think Pirate treasure map!

The first waypoint in a puzzle cache that I solved led me to lamppost. From there I took a bearing and went some distance to another spot where I found the name of a small country on a plate covering pipes in the ground in the park. From that point, I followed directions on the next leg of my journey. Eventually I found a plaque by a bench, and using an encryption code provided, spelled out a word. When I logged in my find, I provided that code word to the person who had set up the cache, and was cleared to add this find to my account..

Puzzles can be tough, requiring many steps. A few geocachers even plant Sudoku puzzles which must be solved first to get the coordinates for the next stage of the cache. These mystery or puzzle caches although hard, can be a lot of fun.

Virtual Caches

Virtual Caches require you to use coordinates to go to a spot, but there is not a physical container and a log book there. You verify that you got to this spot, not by writing in the usual log, but by answering key questions or describing the scene in an email sent to the owner of the cache. The owner then determines if you can be listed as one who Found It! These virtually caches often feature some spectacular views..

Extreme Caches

And there are extreme forms of geocaching caching that involve scuba diving, snorkeling, kayaking or boating, and rock climbing. These forms of geocaching require special training and equipment and are outside the province of this introductory book. But if you have expertise in one or more of these specialized areas, geocaching will be an added bonus to your other sporting activities. Caches that involve such special skills will be so indicated on the geocaching web sites.

At some point, you might want to try to find and to learn about many different kinds of caches. Each is exciting and challenging. The books included in the bibliography will guide you to more detailed information.

Swag or Treasures

Beyond the pleasure of hiding and finding the caches, there's also satisfaction in choosing a special treasure from the cache. These trade items are known as Swag. Except for micro or nanno caches, too small to contain anything but a log sheet, you may choose Swag from the cache you find and leave behind a special treasure for the next geocacher who comes along. You'll want to give some thought to the items you bring with you to leave in the cache. Some people prefer not to take and leave Swag. They simply sign the log book TNLN, meaning took nothing, left nothing..

Generally speaking, if you take something from the cache, you should leave behind something of equal value. Swag for trading is usually of minimal value. It ranges from party-favor toys and fast-food prizes to key chains. sea shells, and foreign coins. A typical cache will have four or five items in it. Most Swag items are worth less than two dollars.

Geocachers have individual styles and Swag sometimes reflects this. They may leave behind a piece of Swag that relates to their handle or geocaching nickname. Battery Boy may always leave behind a small AAA battery. Someone else may always leave a fancy button or a whistle. Others may choose to always leave a foreign coin, a small doll, a toy, a plastic dinosaur, etc. Some bring miscellaneous items and leave the one that best fits into that particular cache. Size is important. If possible, you always bring along a few very small items in case the cache you find simply isn't largest enough to hold your usual favorite leave-behind object. Also, remember that things like power bars or food items, even when wrapped, are not a good idea. They could attract animals that might destroy the cache.

Some geocachers leave a disposable camera in their cache with directions for each finder to snap a picture. The person who planted the cache will check back now and then, replace the camera when its last picture has been used, and may post pictures of the various finders on a web site. Some people take digital pictures of each cache that they find as documentation and as a keepsake of the treasure hunt. Some cache pages have a photo gallery section where you can click

—

and see pictures that others have taken of their hunt.

Hitchhikers

In addition to the usual Swag, a cache may contain a special item known as a hitchhiker. Hitchhikers are trackable items that geocachers move from cache to cache. The most common hitchhikers are travel bugs and geocoins, described below.

Travel Bugs

The best known of the hitchhikers is a travel bug, a name trademarked by Groundspeak, the owner of the website www.geocaching.com. The travel bug usually is an item attached to a dogtag with a number printed on it that is used to track it for geocaching. The bug itself may be a doll, a poker chip, or whatever. These travel bugs are not for keeping. Finders move these objects from cache to cache.

As you grow more experienced in geocaching, you'll probably decide to pick up one of these Travel Bugs from a cache. They are hard to resist! It is easy to learn how to go about picking up and dropping off hitchhikers, and it's fun to keep track of how far and fast they travel.

You can log in any travel bugs that you find on the www.geocaching.com website or on other hitchhiker tracking sites such as Geotag Trackers, (www.travelertags.com,) and Path Tags (www.pathtags.com). Whether you find a Travel Bug and enter it on www.geocaching.com or whether you find another hitchhiker which has a different registration site listed on it, registering these finds allows the person who planted the hitchhiker, and other interested geocachers along the way, to keep track of its travels.

After locating and taking a travel bug, be sure to write down the name and number of the geocache where you found it and the name and tracking number of the travel bug. Go to your computer, and locate trackable items on the appropriate website, Enter the tracking number of the travel bug and fill in the information about where and when you found it, and submit your log entry..

Some travel bugs move about freely traveling far and wide. Others have goals or destinations and are trying to get to a particular spot. Be sure to read about the travel bug on its web page or often on a laminated card attached to it. Try to help it reach its goals. You might be asked by a note attached to the travel bug to take your picture with the bug before sending it along on the next leg of its journey. Any time you take a picture of a travel bug, be careful that its unique number doesn't show. That number should not be revealed unless you are at a geocaching trade show and are sharing the discovery with others.

Later, at another cache, you'll want to drop off the travel bug. Be sure to write down the name and number of the new cache you found where you dropped off the travel bug. When you go to your computer to enter your new geocache finds, go to the page for the cache you just found where you dropped off the travel bug. On www.geocaching.com there is a window near the bottom of that page that lists all the Travel Bugs currently in your possession. Highlight the name of the travel bug that you dropped off at this spot. The cache where you dropped it off will be updated to show that it now holds a travel bug, and the owner of the travel bug will be notified as to its new whereabouts.

As a beginner, you may prefer at first not to pick up a hitchhiker and may instead choose some other item of swag.

—

If you leave the travel bug behind, you can still get credit for discovering the travel bug without actually taking it with you. Make a note of the tracking number on the bug. When you get home to your computer, log in and click on trackable items. Give the information to show that you discovered the travel bug and include in Comments the name of the cache where you saw it. Then submit the log entry. It will be added to your My Account page, and the owner will hear that although it was not retrieved, it was discovered by you. This is also a good option to use when you discover a Travel Bug and you read information at the cache site telling you that this travel bug has a special destination, and you aren't in a position to move it closer to its goal.

Some owners of travel bugs even hold races among themselves to see which can travel from coast to coast first. If you find a travel bug and enter your find on the Internet site, you can also request to be notified as to where this travel bug goes by entering it onto something called a Watch List. For those on your Watch List, each time the travel bug is logged, you will get an email copy of the log notice advising you of the travel bug's current whereabouts. One that I tracked, made its way from Colorado to Canada within two weeks.

Geocoins

Geocoins were devised to be an all-in-one travel bug. They look like coins and range in size from that of a quarter to larger than a silver dollar. Most commemorate cachers or important aspects of geocaching, but anyone can have a coin minted, so the themes on geocoins are as wide ranging as the imagination of cachers. These coins, which vary in size, have a tracking number. When placed and found in a cache, they are treated just like a travel bug. A geocoin found in a cache is not for keeping, unless it is specifically listed as a "First to

—

Find Prize" on the geocaching page.

Some geocoins are never placed in a cache. A person may have an interesting geocoin made, of purchase one for a private collections rather than placing it and watching it travel from cache to cache like travel bugs. Cachers bring their geocoin collections to geocaching events where other coin fans can appreciate them. After the event, the geocachers may "Discover" them, which is to get credit for having seen the coin.

Geocaching.com tracks Discover numbers, just as it tracks how many travel bugs or geocoins a cacher has retrieved and moved from one cache to another. Many geocoins have distinct electronic icons which are posted on the web site and become part of the geocacher's account profile. There are cachers who collect icons attempting to Discover as many unique geocoins as they can.

The first USA Geocoin was put up for sale in 2003. By 2005, a monthly geocoin club was already in business offering subscribers a new coin each month. Today, there are several such clubs. In 2007, hundreds of geocachers attended the First Annual Geocoinfest in Temecula, California where collectors showed off, sold, and traded their coins. Geocoins can be traded through forums, both on geocaching.com and other places. They can be purchased through eBay or directly from many sources. An Internet search on "geocoins" will turn up many dealers and cachers who want to trade coins.

Other Fun Geocaching Items

There are many other sidelights to geocaching. A visit to CafePress.com and searching on "geocaching" will turn up a number of interesting logos that can be placed on everything from t-shirts to coffee cups. Signal the Frog is

---

43

Geocaching.com's mascot, and has his own series of collectible pins. And there are many other accessories and collectibles mentioned on Geocaching.com's advertisements.

While you will be very proud of finding your very first cache and leaving a special piece of Swag behind, alas, you are not yet famous. But you'll probably eventually meet up with people who are, at least they're famous in the world of geocachers. These people have found thousands of caches. Such people might be ranked as one of the top geocachers in yor state or even in the world. These famous people are also tracked! One web site that keeps track of all cachers with 200 or more finds (if among those finds is at least one from some of the popular cache that this web master tracks) can be found at http://www.cacherstats.com.

MOOJOOS the HOLSTEIN COW
(Holland, Europe)
My current goal: This is our B&W series of travel bugs. Nothing is ever as simple as black & white, is it? The mission of each is to make its way to the homeland of its relatives. Visiting other relatives along the way, and taking pictures, is a plus!

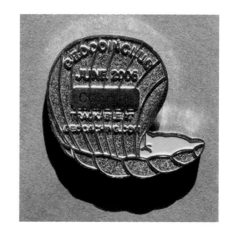

Hiding Your Own Cache

Once you've been on several geocaching hunts, you may decide you want to hide a cache of your own. This allows you to be creative, show off your navigational skills, and add something to this sport that you enjoy. There are just a few basic steps to follow.

1. Carefully read the information about hiding a cache on the geocaching.com web site. It's very specific, but helpful, and will save you grief in the long run.

2. Get a suitable waterproof container. Put inside a pen or pencil and a small log book, perhaps inside another plastic bag to keep out moisture, and add some Swag. Maybe on your hunts you have noticed which types of containers hold

up well in your area, and can choose to use one of those. The toughest of the tough large containers come from an army surplus store.

3. Find a suitable hiding place for your cache. Make sure that it is open to the public. (Sometimes permits must be secured to hide a cache on city park land.) The National Park Services does not allow geocaching on their lands. The Bureau of Land Management, the U.S. Forest Service, and many state and local parks do permit geocaching in lands open to public use. It's your job to find out and to follow rules.) If you place the cache on private property, you must get permission from the owner.

4. Hide the cache. Use common sense. Don't place a cache where people can't safely access it. Don't place it where muggles can't help but notice it. Don't hide a cache in a place that can't stand up to traffic, or in a place where you'll get someone arrested. Be careful to choose a spot that will not put undo stress on the landscape.

5. Take a waypoint. After you hide the cache, take out your GPS receiver and wait until you have a good strong signal. Mark the position. Walk twenty to thirty feet away and approach from another direction. Mark at least three waypoints, and then test your coordinates by walking off a distance and following your waypoint back to the cache. In addition to taking careful coordinates of this spot, also note the difficulty rating you should assign to it both the terrain and the hide itself. (For example, a micro cache in a shrub is almost automatically a 2.5 rating.)

6. When you get home, fill out the cache page form. On geocaching.com, you will need to give it a name, enter its waypoint, and any other information you want to share. Some names are descriptive (Island in the Sky for a huge pile of rocks in a grassy field); some give clues (Troll's Cache for a hiding place near a bridge), and some bear the hider's

name. Geocaching.com's form will also prompt you for cache type, size, attributes (Dogs allowed? Kid friendly? Wheelchair accessible? Poisonous plants?) Other sites will also have specific instructions. When you are satisfied with your information, submit the cache for approval, and wait.

7. After it is submitted, your cache will be reviewed by the local Approver. If your submission passes all the requirements, it will be published. That means the cache is "live" and other geocachers can now go find it. This usually only takes a couple of days. After your cache is posted, whenever it is visited, you will receive a confirmation of the find via email. Follow up on any comments that you might receive from fellow geocachers and visit your site now and then to see that is still there and in good condition. For example, you may need to replace a filled log book.

In hiding your own cache, you are adding greatly to the sport of geocaching and providing for the enjoyment of others.

Mapping Features and Your GPS Receiver

The type and detail of the maps you can use depend on your GPS receiver and its amount of memory. GPS receivers have small screens, so even if you can display maps on your screen, you will only be able to see a small area. For clarity, many geocachers print a map at home on their computer printer and bring it along with them.

When you go to www.geocaching.com and call up a specific cache in which you are interested, you will be given the opportunity to print out a map of the area. If you decide to print maps, you might want to try out several online map options and find out what kind of mapping details work best for you. I like the link: Geocaching.com Google Map. When you zoom in on a map area, you can get a lot of detail. If for example, you are seeking a cache near a residential area, the street names will guide you close to the spot where your intensive search will begin. There may even be a hint to help you, such as, Start near the corner of a street that has the same name as the seventh president of the United States.

You might want to print out a map at home and include the comments from the last five or the last ten cachers. Their comments might contain useful clues. If you are going to be in the woods or wilderness areas, a good map is a necessity. Each country in the world has its own sources for maps of an area. In the United Kingdom, you'd look for an Ordinance Survey, while in France,use its Institut Geographique National. One good U.S. source is the U.S. Geological Survey (USGS). Other sources include the U.S. Forest Service or maps from an outdoor specialty shop in your area.

Topographic Maps

For most caching expeditions near your home, you won't need specialized maps, and, if that's the case, you may skip over this next section. If, however, you are going to be going deep into the woods, you'll need to know how to use topographic maps. A topographic map of an area gives you

---

minute details of physical features, the configuration of the surface including hills and valleys, roads or trails, and any streams or lakes in the area.

Topographic maps have a datum and a grid. The map datum is the set of reference information on which the map is based. In the United States, many maps, including most USGS maps use North American Datum 1927 (NAD27). Newer maps use North American Datum 1983.(NAD83). The geocaching community uses a datum called WGS84. Fortunately for geocachers, WGS84 and NAD83 are the same, and your GPS receiver probably has this as its default setting. Check your GPS receiver manual to be sure of this.

All of this needn't worry you as a beginner except that you must be sure that any map you are using has the same datum as your GPS receiver, because the different datum can make a difference of one-tenth of a mile on the map. If the datum on the map you are using is not North American Datum 1983, you can convert it from one set of coordinates to another. There is a function right on the web site listing of the cache page that will help you do this.

The grid of a topographic map is the set of coordinates that lets you locate spots on the map. The most familiar is latitude and longitude, expressed in degrees and minutes. This is the one you'll probably use. There are other coordinate systems such as UTM, Universal Transverse Mercator; UPS, Universal Polar Stereographic; MGRS, Military Grid Reference System; and a variety of foreign coordinate systems. Most geocaching sites give both latitude and longitude (lat/lon) and the coordinates for UTM. USGS topographic maps feature UTM..

Maps are expensive, and if you are going into a wilderness area with your topographic map, you want to protect your map from dampness. Fold it so that the area in which you're interested is showing out, and carry it in a see-

—

through plastic bag.

You also want to be sure what measuring units you are using. Many GPS receivers receive in metric, statute, and nautical options. If you are most comfortable in working with feet, miles, and miles per hour, be sure to use the statute setting.

Carrying Along a Compass

I seldom use a compass for my geocaching. For most traditional caches, you will need only the website information and your GPS receiver. If you are going out in the woods and have entered into your GPS receiver the spot where you parked your bike or your car as a stored waypoint, your GPS receiver will help you find your way back to that spot

Sometimes, however, a compass is a handy thing to have in reserve, particularly if you are going any distance from a parking lot or trailhead into a wooded or wilderness area. As the old Boy Scout motto says: "Be prepared." Batteries in a GPS could fail. You might get your GPS wet or drop it on a rock. Trees overhead could obscure your view of the sky so that you can't get a good reading. Occasionally Global Positioning System devices around the world are significantly disrupted during a blast of radio waves during a solar flare. In such events, compasses prove to be good, reliable tools. They work indoors or out, in any weather conditions, and are really thrown off only if you are too near metal objects.

Different Kinds of Compasses

There are many kinds of compasses. For general use, the three main types are baseplate, lensatic, and mirrored. For geocaching purposes, you'll probably want to use a baseplate compass, which is particularly useful for working with maps or charts. One of these might cost anywhere between fifteen and a hundred dollars.

On the plate are scales that measure distance on standard types of topographic maps. Around the compass face is a dial marked with the 360 degrees of a circle. These degrees represent the bearing, or azimuth, of its direction in relation to north. If north is at the top of the circle, straight east has a bearing or azimuth of 90 degrees because it is 90 degrees from north on the circle. South has an azimuth of 180 degrees.

This book will not explain how to use a compass on its own or with a topographic map, or how to account for magnetic declination and all the other factors involved in traveling by compass. There are other books for that. Most compasses that you purchase will come with detailed instructions. Becoming proficient with a compass is a desirable skill for the wilderness geocacher.

Other Uses for a GPS

Besides geocaching, you and your family might find other uses for your GPS. If you are out hiking and camping, you might use a GPS to help prevent you from getting lost. You could turn on your GPS receiver and enter as a waypoint the spot where your campsite is located. Later, by turning on your GPS receiver, you would immediately see how far and in what direction your campsite is from where you currently are, so that if you need it, you'll have help in finding your way back.

If you are going on a fishing trip, you can locate a small lake that you want to visit on a topographic map, enter its waypoint into your GPS receiver, and follow the readings on it to lead you to the lake. For backcountry skiers or snowmobilers a GPS a great way to get back to a lodge during a whiteout when snow conditions could be blinding. Mariners were the first people to use the GPS to navigate, and a GPS receiver is still commonly used by sailors on the open seas or in coastal waters.

If your wristwatch should stop or your car clock stops working, your GPS receiver can serve as an accurate clock. If it's turned on while driving in your car, it also gives a very accurate reading of exactly how fast you are driving.

Your leisure time or business activities may also benefit from a GPS. Some golf carts have GPS transmitter/receivers in them to inform players of the distance to the next hole, and the data on each cart can be tracked centrally to see where all the golfers are on a golf course at one time. Commercial and private planes use GPS for navigational purposes through the skies and for directions to runways.

Many industries take advantage of the Global Positioning System. Utility companies use GPS to map such features as gas lines, light poles, cables, and water pipes. Some automobile manufacturers use GPS systems in their cars. This system can tell others where this particular car is and can be used by the driver to locate a particular place that he is seeking or can help police locate a stolen car.

Farming and the forest industry utilize GPS applications, as well as the construction industry. Modern sea floor mapping may combine multibeam echo sounders, GPS, and INS. More and more uses are being found each year for global positioning systems.

Early History and Environmental Awareness

One of the joys of geocaching is being outdoors. However, using the out-of-doors entails some responsibility. It's important both when hiding and seeking a cache that you be environmentally sensitive. You don't want to create unnecessary wear and tear on the land or endanger the habitat of birds and animals. Bad placement of a cache or damage to an area gives the hobby a bad name. This may permanently close-off areas to geocachers.

David J. Ulmer is credited with creating the first cache in the year 2000. He dropped out of the sport about a month later because he was afraid a lot of geocachers would damage our natural world which he valued. Mike Teague is another name associated with the beginning of the sport. He was one of the first to find the original hidden stash, and he developed the first Web site to share and track information about geocaching. Another important name in early geocaching is Jeremy Irish who was a founding partner in Groundspeak, which owns and operates Geocaching.com, the best known of the geocaching Web sites.

From these first founders to today's newcomers, conscientious geocachers are very much aware that large groups of people can cause distress to sensitive environments. They wisely try to create good will toward responsible geocachers. They may join groups to assist in special projects as a sort of "pay back" for using the great out-of-doors. Some of these are called Cache In Trash Out (CITO) events. The time and place for such events are posted on the www.geocaching.com web site. Geocachers gather to pack out litter and trash and to help in trail maintenance, or landscape restoration. Several dozen of these events occur each year and are usually done in conjunction with local parks and recreation departments or with outdoor volunteer organizations.

Social Aspects of Geocaching

Some areas offer social geocaching clubs which may meet in a home, hall, or at a restaurant. The clubs hold social geocaching events where coordinates and a time are given. Interested people gather at a place and bring some food to share. At these events, people exchange tips, help new members, and enjoy meeting fellow geocachers. These event announcements are not for a group hunting of caches but rather are planned get-togethers at an appropriate spot.

Finding a local forum or group of geocachers can be as simple as typing your city name and "geocache" into a search program. Or maybe you'll click through to the owner of a cache you really liked and send an email in which you state you are new to geocaching and would appreciate some tips. You might also watch the geocaching pages for announcements of events in your area of some of their forum topics.

Hazards, Safety, and Common Sense

Responsible geocachers are prepared, put safety first, and

plan ahead to avoid problems. When you go to a geocaching web site, you will usually find a disclaimer, You take on all responsibility and liability when you go geocaching. Clearly you need to use common sense and safety measures at all times. This book provides some simple and basic information, but it is not complex or complete. You could still get into trouble unless you use your head.

What could happen? Unfortunately, a lot of unpleasant things. You could get lost. Knowing how to use a compass and taking one along with you is always a good way to avoid that. Before leaving the parking lot or trail head, entering your current position as a waypoint also helps you find your way back.

You always need to dress appropriately. That means sturdy comfortable shoes suitable for the type of trail you'll be following, the distance, how much you,re carrying with you, etc. The rest of your body also needs good covering, again depending on the length of your trip, terrain, weather, etc. and whether or not you're in an area with ticks, mosquitoes, etc. A hat may make the difference between being comfortable or not.

If you're looking beneath a log or in a hole in the ground or a niche in the rock, it might be wise to poke about with a stick first, instead of putting your hand or foot inside and finding some creature is living there. You're not looking for a snake bite! Not to mention angry scorpions, spiders, and red ants. Also watch where you're walking to avoid stepping on an animal, an icy patch of trail, loose rocks, roots, or off a cliff..

Learn to identify poison oak, poison ivy, poison sumac, and bull nettle. Don't blithely go geocaching in the midst of poisonous plants, or you will regret it! Wear insect repellent. Nothing makes a cache hunt less fun than a swarm of mosquitoes. Deer flies, ticks, chiggers--these are a few of the

—

local critters who will spoil your good time if you don't dress appropriately which means long sleeves, long pants, and good shoes. If you're in a tick area, be sure to check yourself carefully afterwards to make sure you haven't carried one home that is burrowing into your skin.

Find out about the weather conditions and the terrain you will be in. If you are a visitor to a mountainous area, high altitude could prove to be a problem for you. Allow time to adjust to high altitude so you won't get altitude sickness. If you get severe headaches, head for lower ground, drink water, and if it's available, you might take an aspirin..

You could also fall or could get caught in a sudden storm. A plastic rain parka doesn't take up a lot of space in a backpack. The temperature may drop suddenly and you could get dangerously cold. You could also get so hot that you could suffer from heat exhaustion of heat stroke. To avoid dehydration, always carry water with you. While geocaching, be aware of how you are feeling and take steps to keep yourself safe and comfortable.

As best you can, expect the unexpected. Before you leave home, certainly let someone know where you are going, so that if you do become hurt or lost, someone will mount a search for you. Taking along some food and water is basic since you may be gone longer than you planned. Also, always carry a pen or pencil to log your find since these could be missing from the cache.

Do you need a hiking aide such as a trekking pole or a walking staff? How about a cell phone and a headlamp or flashlight? Some people never venture out in the woods without a first aid kit, a Swiss army knife, and a whistle. Sun glasses, lip balm, and bug repellent can certainly come in handy. Binoculars and a camera can add to the fun. All of this equipment might be carried in a medium-sized, comfortable pack.

—

Conclusion

While trying to plan ahead for the unexpected, you should also look forward to the expected: a successful outing, a pleasant hunt, and the satisfaction of finding a hidden cache.

Whether you want to find 100 caches a week, or one cache a month, geocaching is a hobby anyone with a GPS receiver, Internet access, and a spirit of adventure can enjoy. All it takes is a mix of beach combing, treasure hunt, James Bond, and CSI. It will take you to things you never suspected around the block or around the country.

It is a wonderful family activity. A four-year-old may be better at finding the micro in the juniper tree than you are! And if you choose to go beyond using billion dollar satellites to find Tupperware in the woods, you will also meet a marvelous group of fellow adventurers, from all walks of life and all abilities.

You'll find the great treasures of geocaching aren't material.

Join the adventure. Join the quest. And in the words of your fellow gamers, Cache on!

63

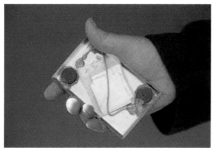

Glossary of Terms

Acquisition Time: The matter of seconds or minutes needed after turning on your GPS receiver to collect information from the satellites to find out its precise location.

Azimuth: Most commonly, the length, in degrees, measured from true North.

Cache: The target package including container and contents (log and small items for trade).

CITO: Cache In Trash Out. Events planned for geocachers to assist local park and forestry groups by helping clean up and preserve land.

Compass: A device used to indicate horizontal direction based on the earth's magnetic field.

Coordinates: A set of numbers and letters that describe a location within a spatial reference system, such as longitude and latitude.

Datum: The horizontal reference system associated with particular coordinates.

D-Con: An army surplus container in which caches are sometimes hidden.

Degree: The measure of distance in a circle from its starting point; a circle contains 360 degrees.

DNF: Short hand for indicating one Did Not Find a cache.

FTF: Short hand for indicating this is the First To Find this cache.

Geocoin: A coin containing a unique ID that people move from geocache to geocache and which might be tracked on the Internet.

GoTo: A function of most GPS receivers that you choose by pressing a dedicated key or selecting it from a menu . When activated, it guides you to a destination until you reach it or cancel it.

GPS: Global Positioning System. Refers to a satellite-based positional system that gives a user's position anywhere on earth. One such system is NAVSTAR.

Grid: Parallel lines on a map that represent a rectangular coordinate system.

International Date Line: A line of longitude located at 180 degrees.

Landmark: A distinctive natural or man-made feature that is found outdoors.

Latitude: The angular distance in degrees of a point north or south of the equator.

Letterboxing: A game similar to Geocaching played in the United Kingdom where a rubber stamp is hidden in a cache. The finder also has a personal stamp. The finder stamps the cache log box with his personal stamp, and also stamps his personal logbook with the stamp from the cache.

Lock: The state when an operating GPS receiver is reading enough satellite signals to calculate a fix.

Logbook: A pad, or pages of paper, in which people who locate a cache sign their name as proof of their discovery.

Longitude: The angular distance in degrees of a point east or west of the Prime Meridian which runs through Greenwich, England

.Magnetic Declination: The difference between true north and magnetic north at a particular location.

Magnetic North: The direction to which the north needle on a compass points in the absence of local magnetic interference.

Map Display/Page: A screen to consult on a GPS receiver that shows a built-in or downloaded map or that shows projected direction and past track.

Meridian: A line of longitude.

Minute: A measurement of distance and a division of one degree; there are 60 minutes in one degree, and sixty seconds in one minute.

Muggle: A person unfamiliar with the game of geocaching. (This term is borrowed from the Harry Potter books.)

Multicache: A geocaching game in which more than one cache box must be found in sequence in order to locate the final cache.

NAD27: North American Datum of 1927 which is used on almost all USGS topographic maps.

NAD83: North American Datum of 1983 which is used on more recent maps produced in the United States and is almost identical to WGS94.

NAVSTAR: The name of the U.S. Department of Defense satellite navigation system that is used by geocachers.

Parallel: A line of latitude.

Position Fix: The coordinates calculated by a GPS receiver by using the signals from at least three satellites.

Prime Meridian: The line of longitude that is assigned a value of zero in a particular horizontal datum. On U.S. maps, the prime meridian passes through Greenwich, England.

Route: In a GPS receiver, a sequential series of waypoints that form a series of legs, or short parts, of the trip.

Scale: The relationship between distance on a map and the distance on the ground it represents.

Swag: The trade items placed in a cache which are taken and replaced by geocachers.

TFTC: Short hand, often used in cache logs to say Thanks for the cache.

TNLN: Short hand often used in cache logs to say, Took nothing, left nothing.

Track Log: The points of your path from the time you turns your GPS receiver on. (Sometimes called a breadcrumb trail.) The entire trail can be made into a route that shows up on your receiver's map page.

Topographic Map: A map with curved lines that represent both horizontal and vertical positions of the features shown.

Travel Bug: This is a metal dog-tag with a number on it that is placed in a cache, picked up by a geocacher and taken to another cache. In this way it travels from one cachet to another with its progress tracked on the Internet. Some travel bugs have specific goals and cachers try to help the travel bug along.

True North: The direction indicated by a line of longitude in the direction of the North Pole.

UPR: Short hand for unnatural pile of rocks which might be a clue that a cache is hidden there.

USGS: United States Geological Survey. A part of the U.S. Department of the Interior. It is the primary mapping agency for the U.S. government.

UTC: Universal Time Coordinated. The time to which all GPS signals are synchronized which is almost identical to Greenwich Mean Time.

Waypoint: A representation of a point on earth that is stored in a GPS receiver in the form of precise geographic coordinates.

YAPIDKA: Short hand, often used in a cache log to say, Yet another park I didn't know about.

Bibliography

Dyer, Mike. The Essential Guide to Geocaching: Tracking Treasure with your GPS. Golden, CO: Fulcrum, 2004.

El-Rabbany, Ahmed. Introduction to GPS: The Global Positioning System. Boston, Ma: Artech House, 2002.

Featherstone, Steve. Outdoor Guide to Using Your GPS. Chanhassen, MN: Creative Publishing, International, 2004.

Ferguson, Michael. GPS Land Navigation: A Complete Guidebook for Backcountry Users of the NAVSTAR Satellite System, Boise, Idaho: Glassford Publishing, 1997.

Letham, Lawrence. UPS Made Easy: Using Global Positioning Systems in the Outdoors. (2nd ed.) Seattle, WA: The Mountaineers, 1998.

Basic Map Skills Booklet. National Geographic Maps. Evergreen, CO: National Geographic, 2003.

Rosinsky, Natalie M. Satellites and the GPS. Minneapolis, MN: Compass Point Books, 2004.

Sherman, Eric. Geocaching: Hide and Seek With Your GPS. Berkeley, CA: Apress, distributed by Springer-Verlag, New York, 2004.

Other Resources

Web sites:

www.geocaching.com

The official site for the geocache game worldwide.

www.mapblast.com

A search engine that supplies most of the maps used on Geocaching.com.

www.nationalgeographic.com/mapmachine

A free, searchable of topographic maps of the United States.

www.mapquest.com

Online road maps to help you find your way to a park, trailhead, etc.

www.terracaching.com

A geocaching web site.

Galileo World magazine

http://www.galileosworld.com/

GPS World magazine.

http://www.gpsworld.com/

Useful Addresses for Sources of Geocaching Materials

Brunton

620 E. Monroe Avenue

Riverton, WY 82501

http://www.brunton.com

Cobra Electronics Corporation

6500 W. Cortland Street

Chicago, IL 60707

www.cobra.com

DeLorme

Two DeLorme Drive

P.O. Box 298

Yarmouth, ME 04096

www.delorme.com

Freeflight Systems

3700 I-35

Waco, TX 76706

Fugawi, Northport Systems, Inc.

95 St. Clair Avenue W., Suite 106

Toronto, Ontario

M4V IN6 Canada

www.fugawi.com

Garmin USA

1200 E. 151st Street

Olathe, KS 66062

www.garmin.com

GPS Outfitters

P.O. Box 237

Stephens City, VA 22655

http://gpsoutfitters.com

Lowrance Electronics

12000 E. Skelly Drive

Tulsa, OK 74128

Magellan Systems Corporation

960 Overland Court

San Dimas, CA 91773

wwwmagellengps.com

Maptech

10 Industrial Way

Amesbury, MA 01913

www.maptech.com

National Geographic Maps

P.O. Box 4537

Evergreen, CO 80437-4357

www.nationalgeographic.com

National Oceanic and Atmospheric Administration

14th Street & Constitution Ave., NW

Room 6217

Washington, D.C. 20230

www.noaa.gov

NovAtel, Inc.

1120 68th Ave., NE

Calgary, Alberta T2E 9S5

Canada

gps@novatel.ca

Pharos Science and Applications

411 Amapola Drive

Torrance, CA 90501

www.pharosgps.com

Suunto

2151 Las Palmas Drive, Suite F

Carlsbad, CA 92011

www.suunto.com

U.S. Geological Survey Headquarters

John W. Powell Federal Building

12201 Sunrise Valley Drive

Reston, VA 20192

www.usgs.gov

About the Author

Phyllis J. Perry is an award winning author of almost 80 published books of fiction and nonfiction for adults and children. She grew up in northern California, attended U. C. Berkeley, and now lives in Boulder, Colorado.

Perry's books are available in many bookstores, and she has twelve titles on the Amazon.com Kindle Book Shelf.

She can be contacted through her web site: www.phyllisperry.com.